GREAT NATIONAL
SOCCER TEAMS

Annie Leah Sommers

WORLD
SOCCER
BOOKS ™

rosen publishing's
rosen
central®

New York

to d.c.

Published in 2010 by The Rosen Publishing Group, Inc.
29 East 21st Street, New York, NY 10010

First Edition

Library of Congress Cataloging-in-Publication Data

Sommers, Annie Leah, 1968–
Great national soccer teams / Annie Leah Sommers.—1st ed.
    p. cm.—(World soccer books)
Includes bibliographical references and index.
ISBN 978-1-4358-9138-8 (library binding)
ISBN 978-1-61532-873-4 (pbk)
ISBN 978-1-61532-874-1 (6 pack)
1. Soccer teams—Miscellanea—Juvenile literature. 2. Soccer—Miscellanea—Juvenile literature.
I. Title.
GV943.25 .S66
796.334—dc22

2009021087

Manufactured in China

CPSIA Compliance Information: Batch #HW10YA: For Further Information contact Rosen Publishing, New York, New York at 1-800-237-9932

On the cover: Top: After defeating Nigeria in the World Youth Championship final in 2005, the Argentine team hoists their trophy amid a storm of confetti. Bottom: The French team poses for photographs after beating Brazil by a score of 3–0 in the 1998 World Cup final.

CONTENTS

INTRODUCTION

Variations of soccer have been played throughout the world for centuries. Part of the beauty of the game is that it can be played anywhere—the only requirements are a ball, enough players to make up two opposing teams, and an area to play in. Historians have traced the game's beginnings back to the second century BCE in China. Back then, using their feet only, men kicked around a leather ball filled with feathers and hair. From East Asia, the game spread to ancient Greece, where, for the first time, the game was played on a rectangular field.

Modern soccer as we know it emerged in 19th-century England, where official rules were drawn up to govern the sport. At the time, Britain's global empire was at its peak, and the game was quickly adopted in many countries around the world: from Canada and Kenya to Australia and India. Today, soccer is the most popular sport in the world. At present, more than 52 million soccer players throughout the world take part in official competition. Passion for the game is spreading rapidly, and more countries than ever have transformed their growing soccer enthusiasm into highly skilled and competitive national teams.

As international soccer mania has expanded, new national soccer teams have risen to world prominence. Traditional soccer powerhouses, such as Brazil, Argentina, Italy, and Germany, face stiff competition from up-and-coming national teams, such as Cameroon and Nigeria. Talented players, such as Cameroon's Samuel Eto'o, Nigeria's Augustine Azuka "Jay-Jay" Okocha, and the United States' Landon Donovan, have risen to prominence in the sport.

Soccer fans are as passionate about the sport as the people who play it. Around the world, fans fill stadiums, wear the colors of their

On May 15, 2004, citizens of Capetown, South Africa, cheer with joy at FIFA president Sepp Blatter's announcement that South Africa has earned the right to host World Cup 2010.

favorite team, tune into daily soccer results, and follow their team on soccer Web sites and blogs. If interest in the World Cup is a measure of the popularity of the game, the 2010 World Cup in South Africa will be the most-watched international soccer tournament to date. By the end of March 2009, the Web site for the Fédération Internationale de Football Association (FIFA) had received more than one million online ticket applications, from 150 different countries, for the 2010 World Cup. This is but one indication that soccer will remain the most popular sport in the world for some time to come.

CHAPTER 1

ARGENTINA:
PURE SKILL

In Argentina, British and Italian residents encouraged the formation of South America's first soccer team, Buenos Aires, in 1865. The first league in South America was set up 28 years later. Argentina currently holds the world record for the most international titles won by a national team. The two-time World Cup champions (1978 and 1986) were also gold medal winners at both the 2004 and 2008 Olympic Games.

Argentina's soccer dominance was brought about in no small part by amazing coaching. Foremost among Argentina's coaches was Cesar Luis Menotti, a former player who became the head coach of Argentina before the 1978 World Cup. Menotti revolutionized Argentina's soccer team, instructing his players to relentlessly focus on scoring. He coached the team until 1992, leaving an indelible mark on Argentina's style of play.

ARGENTINA'S FINEST PLAYERS

Argentina has fielded some of soccer's most legendary players. The most famous person ever to play for Argentina was Diego Maradona, who was born in Buenos Aires in 1960. His magician-like control of the ball was

NICKNAME:
ALBICELESTES (WHITE AND SKY BLUE)

FEDERATION:
ARGENTINE FOOTBALL ASSOCIATION (AFA)

FOUNDED:
1893

JOINED FIFA:
1912

HONORS:
FIFA WORLD CUP
APPEARANCES: 14
WINS: 2 (1978, 1986)

COPA AMERICA
WINS: 14 (1921, 1925, 1927, 1929, 1937, 1941, 1945, 1946, 1947, 1955, 1957, 1959, 1991, 1993)

FIFA CONFEDERATIONS CUP
WINS: 1 (1992)

FIFA U-20 WORLD CUP
WINS: 6 (1979, 1995, 1997, 2001, 2005, 2007)

enchanting to watch. He began his career at the young age of 15, playing club soccer for the Argentinos Juniors.

The great striker became a legend after his star turn in the 1986 World Cup, where he led the team to a 3–2 victory over West Germany in Mexico's Azteca Stadium. As brilliant a player as Maradona was, he was also somewhat of a controversial figure. Though he had been the captain of the national team in the 1990 World Cup, he failed a drug test in 1991 and was banned from the game for 15 months. Four years later, Maradona was sent home from the World Cup after testing positive for the stimulant ephedrine. Maradona battled his drug addiction and came back to claim the illustrious honor of sharing FIFA's Footballer of the Century Award in 2000 with Pelé, the legendary Brazilian player. Maradona came back to coach Argentina in 2008 in preparation for World Cup 2010.

One of Maradona's most legendary goals in an international game occurred at the 1986 World Cup, in the quarterfinal match against England. Tensions were high, as it was the first time the countries had met since fighting each other in the 1982 Falklands War. In the second half, Maradona appeared to miraculously head the ball into the goal past British goalkeeper Peter Shilton as the two collided. After a moment of uncertainty, the goal was called. When asked about the goal after the game, Maradona displayed his characteristic charm by saying that the "hand of God" had put the goal in the net. He had actually hit the ball with his hand, but the officials did not see him do so. They didn't call a violation and let the goal stand.

Four minutes later, Maradona struck again. Taking the ball in his own half, Maradona started a 196-foot (60 meter) sprint toward the goal. Maradona left behind five English players and finished by

Champion scorer Lionel Messi (#18) lets loose with fellow teammates after Argentina scored the first goal against Colombia at the World Cup South Africa 2010 qualifying match in Bogotá, Colombia.

Argentine powerhouse Diego Maradona competes at the 1986 World Cup semifinals against Belgium. The match took place in front of more than 100,000 fans at Azteca Stadium in Mexico City.

dribbling past the goalie and kicking the ball to the net. This goal was so spectacular that it has been called the "Goal of the Century."

The person generally considered to be Maradona's successor is a young Argentine named Lionel Messi, who made his debut at the age of 16 in 2003. A talented player who is a key component of Argentina's offense, Messi is a skilled ball handler who is particularly good at facing down defenders. It appears that he is destined to join the ranks of the great players. Along with relative newcomers, such as striker Sergio "Kun" Agüero, and legends like striker Mario Kempes and defender Daniel Passarella, Messi is helping to make Argentina a global soccer superpower.

CHAPTER 2

BRAZIL:
THE BEAUTIFUL GAME

Soccer is a popular phenomenon in Brazil. You can nearly feel it in the air. In fact, it's hard to find a Brazilian who doesn't have an opinion on the latest soccer match, his or her favorite team, a coach's wrong call, or a star player's personal life. Soccer is an integral part of Brazil's culture and is taken very seriously. Brazilian soccer is known for its free, open, almost dancelike style, referred to as "the beautiful game" because of its fluidity and the sheer majesty of its tactical skill.

Popular myth has it that the game was brought to Brazil by a young man named Charles Miller. Miller was born in Brazil and was sent to school in England. When Miller returned to the city of São Paulo in 1884, he brought two soccer balls back with him. He then went about converting cricket-playing British expatriates to the thrills of the game he had seen abroad. In 1884, the first football club, the São Paulo Athletic Club, was founded. The game soon began to spread throughout Brazil. By the early part of the 20th century, the public and the media had caught on to the thrill of soccer. Unlike other popular sports of the time, such as tennis

NICKNAME:
VERDE E AMARELA
(GREEN AND YELLOW)

FEDERATION:
BRAZILIAN FOOTBALL
CONFEDERATION (CBF)

FOUNDED:
1914

JOINED FIFA:
1923

HONORS:
FIFA WORLD CUP
APPEARANCES: 18
WINS: 5 (1958, 1962, 1970,
1994, 2002)

COPA AMÉRICA
WINS: 8 (1919, 1922, 1949,
1989, 1997, 1999, 2004, 2007)

FIFA CONFEDERATIONS CUP
WINS: 2 (1997, 2005)

FIFA U-20 WORLD CUP
WINS: 4 (1983, 1985,
1993, 2003)

**FIFA U-17 WORLD CUP/
COPA MUNDIAL FIFA SUB-17**
WINS: 3 (1997, 1999, 2003)

and cricket, soccer could be played by anyone: all you needed was a ball.

WORLD CUP WONDERS

The Brazilian team is famous for its astounding number of wins in international competition. Brazil has won five World Cup championships—more than any other country in the world! After its extraordinary 1970 World Cup win, Brazil became the first country to win the World Cup three times. After this, Brazil was

The Brazilian team claims the 2002 World Cup championship in Yokohama, Japan. Brazil beat Germany 2–0 in the final match to claim their fifth championship.

given the Jules Rimet Trophy (awarded to World Cup champions) to keep forever!

The Brazilian team that competed in the 1970 World Cup tournament is considered to be one of the best ever. It included soccer legends such as Pelé, defender Carlos Alberto Torres, winger Jair Ventura "Jairzinho" Filho, striker Eduardo "Tostão" Gonçalves de Andrade, and midfielder Roberto Rivelino. The great attacking flair of Rivelino, the scoring success of Jairzinho, and the sheer

beauty of Pelé's poetic, tactical play proved to international soccer fans that Brazil was a serious force to be reckoned with. The Brazilian style of play—both improvisational and free-flowing—makes Brazil one of the most thrilling soccer teams in the world to watch.

MARACANÃ

Rio de Janeiro's famed Maracanã stadium has been home to some great moments in the history of the country's national team. It was there that a young Pelé scored his first international goal at age 15, as well as being where his 1,000th career goal took place. Brazilian fans respond to soccer and its players with displays of high emotions. During games, fans sing popular carnival songs and samba in the aisles of the Maracanã. At the 1950 World Cup, nearly 200,000 fans watched as the Brazilian team lost the final by a score of 2–1 against Uruguay. The moment went down in history as the "final fatidica," or the fateful final. Everyone was so shocked by the loss that the stadium was silent, and the announcer had to repeat the score three times.

The legendary Pelé hoists the Jules Rimet Trophy on June 21, 1970, after Brazil beat Italy to claim their second World Cup championship.

CAMEROON: THE POWERHOUSE

T

he history of soccer in Cameroon dates back to its colonization, when the game was part of the sports curriculum in British-run schools. British colonists and local Cameroonians became soccer enthusiasts, and eventually, several football clubs were formed. The official governing body of African Football, the Confédération Africaine de Football (Confederation of African Football, or CAF), was founded in 1957. Since then, soccer has become one of the most popular sports in Cameroon.

The Cameroon team, often referred to as the Indomitable Lions, is one of the best in the world.

THE LIONS ROAR

Cameroon has participated in the World Cup five times, and in 1990, the team reached the quarterfinals. The team's best performance came during the 2000 Olympics in Sydney. Another African soccer team, Ghana, was the favorite to win the gold. However, the Cameroon team coach, Jean Paul Akono, had built a formidable team. His recipe for success: mixing the tried-and-true skills of seasoned players, like striker Patrick Mboma and defender Serge Mimpo, with a

NICKNAME:
LIONS INDOMPTABLE (INDOMITABLE LIONS)

FEDERATION:
CAMEROON FOOTBALL FEDERATION (FECAFOOT)

FOUNDED:
1959

JOINED FIFA:
1962

HONORS:
FIFA WORLD CUP
APPEARANCES: 5
QUARTERFINALIST
IN 1990

AFRICAN CUP OF NATIONS
WINS: 4 (1984, 1988, 2000, 2002)

FIFA CONFEDERATIONS CUP
APPEARANCES: 2
RUNNERS-UP: 2003

OLYMPIC MEDAL RECORD
GOLD: 2000 SYDNEY

CHAPTER 3

Perhaps the best striker in soccer today, Cameroon's Samuel Eto'o is seen here at a 2003 Confederations Cup match in France.

young crew of up-and-coming stars, such as striker Samuel Eto'o and defender Lauren Etame Mayer.

During the tournament, it became obvious that Cameroon was playing to win. The team beat a stunned Brazil 2–1 in the quarterfinals, after Patrick Mboma came off the bench to score a goal in overtime. This goal made Mboma a national hero in Cameroon. In the semifinal game against Chile, Mboma scored once again, advancing Cameroon to the finals for the first time in Olympic history. The team kept its edge in the final match against Spain, where Cameroon won Olympic Gold in front of a roaring audience.

Cameroon's soccer stars pose for the press before the second phase of the World Cup finals in Naples, Italy, on June 23, 1990.

The national team has a brilliant record at the African Cup of Nations, with wins in 1984, 1988, 2000, and 2002. At the 1984 tournament in the Ivory Coast, Cameroon faced Nigeria in the final. The Indomitable Lions scored two late goals to win the trophy for the first time. In the final match in the 2000 African Cup of Nations, Cameroon beat Nigeria once again in a dramatic match. Things seemed to be going smoothly for Cameroon after goals by Samuel Eto'o and Patrick Mboma gave them a 2–0 lead. Nigeria rallied, tying the game up with two goals. Fans held their breath until defender Rigobert Song scored the winning goal, putting Cameroon over the top and winning them the championship.

SAMUEL ETO'O

Samuel Eto'o is considered to be one of the best strikers in world soccer. Eto'o's versatility, quickness, and excellent control of the ball allowed him to join Cameroon's national team at the young age of 15. Eto'o was only 16 (and didn't speak a word of Spanish) when Real Madrid signed him up in 1997. The following year, he was the youngest player at the 1998 World Cup in France.

Eto'o's honors don't stop there. Often at the top of "best of" lists, he was named African Footballer of the Year in 2003, 2004, and 2005. Eto'o was also one of the three finalists for the 2005 FIFA World Player of the Year. In 2007, the CAF placed him in the top five when it named the 30 best African players in the last 50 years. Cameroon soccer legend Roger Milla headed the list.

MARC-VIVIEN FOE

Cameroon midfielder Marc-Vivien Foe had an immensely successful career in Africa and Europe, and is especially remembered for his debut at World Cup USA in 1994. A national hero, Foe represented Cameroon in four African Cup of Nations finals. The soccer world was heartbroken by Foe's sudden death, due to a heart condition, at the young age of 28. Foe collapsed during the semifinal game against Colombia in the FIFA Confederations Cup in France in 2003.

CHAPTER 4

ENGLAND:
THE ORIGINATORS

The history of modern soccer began in England more than 140 years ago when the Football Association was founded on October 26, 1863. Until this time, two different styles of the game had been played: a full-contact, ball-carrying style called rugby, and a more moderate style known as football. Football was popular, and educators felt the virtues the game inspired—loyalty and self-discipline—were vital to the moral and spiritual growth of young men.

In 1846, Dr. Thomas Arnold, the head of the Rugby School, unsuccessfully tried to standardize a set of rules for organized school games. Not pleased with the results, some Cambridge University students tried to sort out the confusion in 1848. Eventually, 11 clubs and schools sent representatives to the Freemason's Tavern on October 26, 1863, to establish one fixed set of rules. On December 8 of the same year, football and rugby split into two different sports.

The meeting at the tavern led to the creation of soccer's first governing body, the Football Association. Under the direction of Ebenezer Cobb Morley, the original 17 laws—known as the Laws of the Game—were written up. Eventually, these laws (which are now revised by FIFA) would govern the most popular sport on the planet.

The first international match was played in 1872 between England and

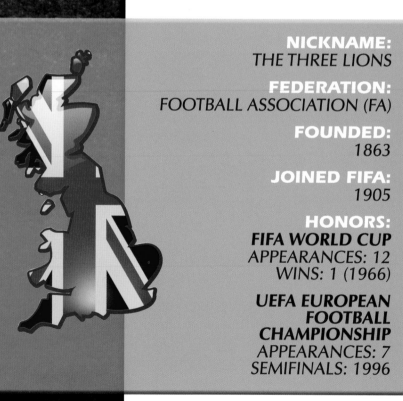

NICKNAME:
THE THREE LIONS

FEDERATION:
FOOTBALL ASSOCIATION (FA)

FOUNDED:
1863

JOINED FIFA:
1905

HONORS:
FIFA WORLD CUP
APPEARANCES: 12
WINS: 1 (1966)

UEFA EUROPEAN FOOTBALL CHAMPIONSHIP
APPEARANCES: 7
SEMIFINALS: 1996

The Bolton Wanderers, seen here in a photo from the early 1880s, were one of the founding members of Britain's Football League. They are still going strong today.

Scotland. When FIFA was formed in 1904, the United Kingdom was initially put out that an international organization was being established according to British rules. Ultimately, however, the world recognized the immense value of Britain's contribution to soccer.

THE CHAMPIONS

England's national team started off the 20th century with a bang, claiming back-to-back Olympic gold medals at the 1908 games in London and the 1912 games at Stockholm. Britain's biggest claim to fame, however, was the team's victory at the 1966 World Cup.

Going into the tournament, the Brits were in top form due to the talent of coach Alf Ramsey. Coach Ramsey trained the team to be quick on defense and efficient on offense. Bobby Charlton was the offensive star of the British team. With the defensive wizardry of Bobby Moore and the unexpectedly explosive speed of striker Geoff Hurst, the British team was a far stronger one than the West Germans had bargained for. Ramsey's motivational coaching prompted Hurst to score the winning goal—his third of the match. Hurst became the first ever player to record a hat trick in the final match.

CONTINUING EXCELLENCE

In recognition of his soccer excellence, which included being named European Footballer of the Year in 1966, top-goal-scorer Bobby Charlton was knighted in 1994. More than a decade later, on March 2, 2009, Charlton was awarded the Freedom of the City (an award that is similar to the Key to the City in the United States) of Manchester for his brilliant career with both the national team and Manchester United.

David Beckham recently beat out Charlton to become England's third most capped player ever. On March 28, 2009, Beckham hit his 109th cap, thereby surpassing Bobby Moore's record of 108 caps for an outfield player. At this point, it's safe to say that it won't be that far into the future before Beckham will have broken the current record: Peter Shilton's jaw-dropping 125 caps for England.

A team of legends, England defeated West Germany to win the 1966 FIFA World Cup championship. Bobby Moore is standing third from the left in the top row, and Bobby Charlton is third from the left on the bottom row.

FRANCE: SOCCER MAGIC

The Fédération Internationale de Football Association (FIFA) was founded in Paris on May 21, 1904, marking the debut of professional soccer in France. After soccer was featured in the 1908 and 1912 Olympic games, FIFA decided to hold its own world championship. By 1913, South Africa, Argentina, Chile, and the United States had joined France in the creation of an international soccer competition. Jules Rimet was appointed chairman of the board of FIFA in Antwerp, Belgium, in 1920. After becoming FIFA's third president in 1921, Rimet masterfully steered FIFA during the next 33 years of his presidency. During this time, FIFA's membership grew substantially. By 1954, 85 countries had joined the federation.

The French team eventually claimed World Cup victory in 1998 and introduced some of soccer's brightest stars to the game, including Michel Platini and Zinédine "Zizou" Zidane. Though Zidane retired after leading France to a second-place finish at World Cup 2006, sports journalists are wondering if up-and-coming French players Samir Nasri and left-winger Hatem Ben Arfa will take over the reins, ushering in a new generation of promising and supremely talented soccer players.

NICKNAME:
LES BLEUS (THE BLUES)

FEDERATION:
FRENCH FOOTBALL FEDERATION (FFF)

FOUNDED:
1919

JOINED FIFA:
1907

HONORS:
FIFA WORLD CUP
APPEARANCES: 12
WINS: 1 (1998)

UEFA EUROPEAN FOOTBALL CHAMPIONSHIP
APPEARANCES: 7
WINS: 2 (1984, 2000)

FIFA CONFEDERATIONS CUP
WINS: 2 (2001, 2003)

FIFA U-17 WORLD CUP
WINS: 1 (2001)

OLYMPIC MEDAL RECORD
GOLD: 1984 LOS ANGELES
SILVER: 1900 PARIS

French star Alain Giresse takes command of the ball during the 1998 UEFA championship final in Paris.

IMPORTANT CHAMPIONSHIPS AND GAMES

Les Bleus have quite a history as winners. The team won the 1984 UEFA European Cup tournament, which was held in France, and the 2000 UEFA Cup tournament, which was cohosted by Belgium and the Netherlands. Star players of the team in 2000 included striker Thierry Henry and the dazzling midfielder Zidane. The team also brought home an Olympic gold at the 1984 games in Los Angeles. One of France's most significant wins was against the masterful Brazilians at the 1998 World Cup.

THE STARS OF THE 1984 UEFA CUP

A famous victory for the French national team occurred at the 1984 UEFA Cup when France defeated Spain in the final at Parc des Princes stadium in Paris. Dominating the

Hundreds of thousands of joyous fans participate in a victory parade in Paris, celebrating France's 1998 World Cup triumph over Brazil.

tournament with their formidable soccer finesse, the French won all their matches. Crucial to their victories was the top-notch talent of goalkeeper Joel Bats, along with the deft scoring of team mastermind Michel Platini. Platini and the other midfielders on the team—Luis Fernandez, Alain Giresse, and Jean Tigana—became known as *Le Carré Magique*, or the "Magic Square." They were an integral part of France's success. Platini's goal in the final marked his ninth goal of the Cup, and he led France to a 2–0 victory. Platini was also the tournament's top scorer.

WORLD CUP 1998

The final match of the 1998 World Cup will go down in history as one of the most well-remembered games in international soccer. Expectations for the French were not high, as they had never before advanced to a World Cup final. They were also facing off against soccer titans Brazil.

France managed to overcome the odds, thanks to the abilities of French superhero Zidane. France was also helped by the fact that star Brazilian striker Ronaldo Luís Nazário de Lima's performance was inhibited from pain medication he was taking for an ankle injury. France ended up beating the Brazilians by a score of 3–0.

THIERRY HENRY

Considered to be one of the best strikers in the world, Thierry Henry was born on August 17, 1977, in a suburb of Paris. He started playing club soccer at the age of 13 and went on to become France's top scorer in the 1998 World Cup and the 2000 UEFA Cup. By early 2008, Henry had surpassed Michel Platini in the number of goals scored.

GERMANY: DISCIPLINE AND HARD WORK

In 1900 in the city of Leipzig, select members of nearly 90 German soccer clubs gathered for an important meeting at a restaurant called Mariengarten. This meeting marked the founding of the German Football Association (DBF). The DBF's first organized game was played in 1908. From 1949 to 1990, Germany was divided into two countries: socialist East Germany and democratic West Germany. The West German team, with its legendary players and effective style, became one of the most respected teams in Europe.

The two Germanies were reunited in 1990. Germany has participated in the World Cup finals an utterly remarkable seven times—and claimed three championships. The most recent win came in 1990, when coach Franz Beckenbauer led the team to victory. Just 16 years earlier, Beckenbauer had helped Germany win the cup as a player. The team has also played in 9 out of 12 UEFA Cup tournaments.

A FORCE TO BE RECKONED WITH

The West German soccer team was a force to be reckoned with. At the 1954 World Cup in Switzerland, West Germany beat the favored team, Hungary, for the championship trophy. Twenty years later, West Germany proudly triumphed over the Netherlands in the dramatic 1974 World Cup

NICKNAME:
DIE MANNSCHAFT
(THE TEAM)

FEDERATION:
THE GERMAN FOOTBALL FEDERATION (DFB)

FOUNDED:
1900

JOINED FIFA:
1904

HONORS:
FIFA WORLD CUP
APPEARANCES: 16
WINS: 3 (1954, 1974, 1990)

UEFA EUROPEAN FOOTBALL CHAMPIONSHIP
APPEARANCES: 10
WINS: 3 (1972, 1980, 1996)

FIFA U-20 WORLD CUP
WINS: 1 (1981)

West German captain Franz Beckenbauer goes up against Holland's John Neeskins during the 1974 World Cup final in Munich, Germany.

finals in Hamburg. The West Germans were headed by sweeper Franz Beckenbauer, the unstoppable and fearsome scorer Gerd Müller, and goalkeeper Sepp Maier, who is remembered for his lightning-quick reflexes and goal-stopping prowess.

The West Germans were victorious once again in an unforgettable final against Argentina in the 1990 World Cup in Italy. They also won UEFA Cup championships in 1972 and 1980. After Germany reunited, the German team won another championship in 1996. One-time U-20 World Cup champions, the West German team hoisted the U-20 trophy in 1981 after a grueling championship match against Qatar.

The German team celebrates their dramatic 1–0 win against Argentina at the 1990 World Cup final in Rome, Italy.

STAR PLAYER: FRANZ BECKENBAUER

Franz Beckenbauer, who is nicknamed "der Kaiser" (the Emperor), is known as one of the finest soccer players in history. Born in 1945, Beckenbauer started playing soccer with a youth team in Munich. He made his debut with the Bayern Munich club in 1964. After winning the German Cup in 1966 and 1967, he led his team to the European Cup championships in 1974, 1975, and 1976.

Beckenbauer's great defensive style and his skill in attacking the ball helped build the fierce reputation of the West Germans. During the time he played for the West German national team, from 1963 to 1977, Beckenbauer helped revolutionize the position that became known as the "sweeper"—a defensive specialist who plays behind other defenders.

After West Germany's 2–1 victory over the Netherlands in the 1974 World Cup finals, Beckenbauer became the first team captain to lift the new FIFA World Cup Trophy, created to replace the Jules Rimet Trophy that had been awarded to Brazil in 1970.

TEAM STARS

The German team is known for their athleticism, pragmatism, efficiency, and well-rounded style of play. This deadly combination has produced excellent defenders, such as defensive midfielder Lothar Matthäus. It has also produced talented goalkeepers, such as Oliver Khan. Khan, who was known as "King Khan," won the Golden Ball (an award given to the best soccer player of the year by *France Football* magazine) due to his performance in the 2002 Korea/Japan final against Brazil. Another giant is the team's former goal-getting top gun, Gerhard "Gerd" Müller, who was responsible for the goal that won the 1974 World Cup.

CHAPTER 7

ITALY: MASTERS OF DEFENSE

Italy's national football team is controlled by the Federazione Italiana Giuoco Calcio (FIGC), which represents the country in international soccer tournaments. The proud winners of four World Cup titles, they rank just behind Brazil as being the most successful soccer team in the history of the game. The team's honors include one European championship title in 1968 and an Olympic gold medal in 1936. Their nickname, "Azzuri," refers to the azure color of their home jerseys.

The Italian team is known for their supremely successful defensive style of soccer. The team takes a somewhat conservative approach to the game, enhanced by the craftsmanship of a number of brilliant players. One of the team's most memorable championships took place at the 1982 World Cup in Spain, where striker Paolo Rossi carried the team to a 3–1 win against West Germany. He was the tournament's top scorer, and his heroics earned him the title of European Footballer of the Year. Another key player in the tournament was Dino Zoff, the crafty and experienced team captain and goalkeeper. Forty-year-old Zoff's on-field accomplishments were honored when King Juan Carlos of Spain presented him with the World Cup Trophy.

Italy has won four World Cup championships, only one less than Brazil. Italy could have won an additional championship in

NICKNAME:
AZZURRI (AZURE)

FEDERATION:
ITALIAN FOOTBALL FEDERATION (FIGC)

FOUNDED:
1898

JOINED FIFA:
1905

HONORS:
FIFA WORLD CUP
APPEARANCES: 16
WINS: 4 (1934, 1938, 1982, 2006)

UEFA EUROPEAN FOOTBALL CHAMPIONSHIP
APPEARANCES: 7
WINS: 1 (1968)

OLYMPIC MEDAL RECORD
GOLD: 1936 BERLIN
BRONZE: 1928 AMSTERDAM AND 2004 ATHENS

After an exciting final match between Italy and France, goalkeeper Gianluigi Buffon (center) is mobbed by his fellow teammates. Buffon blocked a penalty kick, allowing Italy to claim victory.

1994 if it hadn't been for a single missed shot. Italy faced Brazil in the 1994 World Cup final. These teams, the best in the world, had ended the game with a 0–0 tie—the first time this had happened in World Cup history. Striker Roberto Baggio was about to take Italy's fifth penalty kick, and pressure was high. Because Brazilian goalie Cláudio Taffarel had a tendency to dive to one side of the net, Baggio decided to send the ball straight

The Italian national soccer team poses for a group photo on June 10, 1934, right before facing off against Czechoslovakia (now the Czech Republic) in the World Cup final. Italy would go on to beat their rivals 2–1 in extra time.

down the middle. However, he shot the ball over the goal and missed. This miss caused Italy to lose the World Cup. Italy had to wait until 2006 to win another World Cup.

ITALIAN SOCCER IN THE 1930S

The Italian soccer team not only won the Olympic gold in 1936, but they also won World Cup championships in 1934 and 1938. FIFA decided that the second World Cup would be hosted by Italy in 1934. This was a somewhat controversial decision, as Italy was ruled by the fascist dictator Benito Mussolini at the time. Some feared that Mussolini would use the World Cup to promote his political agenda. Fortunately, the Italian national team triumphed over politics with the aid of legendary coach Vittorio Pozzo.

Pozzo started a soccer revolution when he became coach in 1939. With incredible savvy and a keen eye for talented players, he focused on precision and defensive skill. As a result, Italy won the 1934 World Cup final against Czechoslovakia. Defense leader Luis Monti and Raimondo Orsi, who had polished up the team's offensive skill with creative plays, helped lead the Italian team to victory.

CHAPTER 8

MEXICO: A FORCE TO BE RECKONED WITH

The heyday of Mexican soccer supremacy started in the 1990s, when the national team dominated the Confederation of North, Central America and Caribbean Association Football (CONCACAF) Gold Cup. Although Mexico lost the inaugural Gold Cup tournament to the United States, their longtime rivals, in 1991, they were victorious throughout the rest of the decade. In 1993, they beat the United States 4–0, scoring 18 goals in 5 games. At the 1996 Gold Cup, Mexico triumphed over Brazil 2–0, and the 1998 Gold Cup ended with a 1–0 win against the United States.

In 2003, Mexico beat Brazil in a thrilling game that was decided in over-time. In 1993, Mexico played its first Copa América game in Ecuador. The Mexicans advanced all the way to the final, where they ultimately lost against Argentina. In 2001, they advanced to the Copa América final again, this time against Colombia, the home team. Ultimately, Mexico returned home with the second-place medal. Mexico hosted the 1999 FIFA Confederations Cup, beating the competition and coming away with the trophy.

Mexico won a major victory in the 2005 FIFA U-17 World Cup in Peru,

NICKNAME:
EL TRI (THE TRICOLOR)

FEDERATION:
MEXICAN FOOTBALL FEDERATION (FEMEXFUT)

FOUNDED:
1927

JOINED FIFA:
1929

HONORS:
FIFA WORLD CUP
APPEARANCES: 13
QUARTERFINALS IN
1970 AND 1986

COPA AMÉRICA
RUNNERS-UP:
1993 AND 2001

FIFA CONFEDERATIONS CUP
WINS: 1 (1999)

FIFA U-17 WORLD CUP
WINS: 1 (2005)

GOLD CUP
WINS: 7 (1965, 1971, 1977,
1993, 1996, 1998, 2003)

During the 2005 U-17 World Cup semifinal match against the Netherlands, Mexican superstar Carlos Vela (center) heads the ball past members of the opposing team.

beating the Brazilian team in the final. Captained by Giovani Dos Santos, Mexico played a perfect tactical game. The stars of the game were goalkeeper Sergio Arias, ace striker Carlos Vela, and midfielder César Villaluz.

MEXICO VS. THE UNITED STATES

Games between the United States and Mexico are often tense, stemming from an ongoing soccer rivalry that is serious business in both countries. They have played against

The Mexican national team is seen here in 1986. That year, Mexico became the first country to host the World Cup finals for a second time.

each other 55 times, out of which Mexico has won 30 games! The United States has triumphed over Mexico much less frequently, only racking up 14 wins. Mexican fans support their beloved team through high-spirited encouragement, often resulting in a nation of hoarse soccer fans.

THE FORTRESS OF RESULTS

When a soccer tournament is held in Mexico's notorious Azteca Stadium, it would be fair to say that the home team has an advantage. Azteca is located more than 7,000 feet (2,134 meters) above sea level, up in the mountains framing Mexico City. The stadium has earned its reputation as a "fortress of results." Only one visiting team has ever triumphed over Mexico at a home game, indicating that the high altitude and record-level smog takes a toll on visiting teams. The sole home defeat came when Costa Rica beat their hosts 2–1 in 2002.

Mexico continues to be a major contender in the soccer world. The team has qualified for the FIFA World Cup 13 times, reaching the quarterfinals in 1970 and again in 1986. Mexico has also advanced to the second round of the World Cup in each of the last four tournaments.

CHAPTER 9

THE NETHERLANDS:
TOTAL FOOTBALL

Though the Netherlands has appeared in eight World Cups, they have yet to win one. The Netherlands finished as runners-up in both the 1974 and 1978 tournaments. During this time, the team was at the height of their mastery of a fluid style of play set forth by coach Rinus Michels. Michels, a former center-forward for the club team Ajax, had also played for the national team. The magic formula that made the Netherlands World Cup contenders was known as "total football." Total football involved the players switching positions with stealth and finesse. The constant rotation among the players worked to slyly confuse the opposing team. Total football allowed the Dutch team to gain scoring opportunities as well as advantages in numbers.

Expectations were high as the Oranje went into the 1974 tournament. The crowds were keen to witness what was viewed as the most entertaining style of soccer ever played. Dutch player Johan Cruyff played a brilliant game of back-and-forth with West German superstar Franz Beckenbauer, roaming all over the field in a frenzy. The fans loved it, and the Dutch garnered a reputation for being highly skilled and creative players. Ultimately, however, they lost to West Germany in the final.

NICKNAME:
ORANJE (ORANGE)

FEDERATION:
NETHERLANDS FOOTBALL ASSOCIATION (FIGC)

FOUNDED:
1889

JOINED FIFA:
1904

HONORS:

FIFA WORLD CUP
APPEARANCES: 8
RUNNERS-UP IN
1974 AND 1978

UEFA EUROPEAN FOOTBALL CHAMPIONSHIP
APPEARANCES: 8
WINS: 1 (1988)

OLYMPIC MEDAL RECORD
GOLD: 1936 BERLIN
BRONZE: 1928 AMSTERDAM
AND 2004 ATHENS

Dutch soccer legend Johan Cruyff keeps tight control of the ball during the 1974 championship game against West Germany.

Total football propelled the Dutch into the spotlight. They were widely considered the favorite going into the 1978 World Cup in Argentina. However, the team's tactics changed under the direction of new coach Ernst Happel. Happel chose to focus on the team's speed and power. The Netherlands were doing well against Argentina until they lost their cool with two uncharacteristic fouls, setting the game into an offensive flurry. Though the Dutch increased pressure in the second half, the Argentine team held steady

Former Dutch coach Rinus Michels leads a 1979 Los Angeles Aztecs practice. Many players and coaches join soccer clubs abroad while maintaining their place on the national team of their home country.

into overtime, where two successive goals resulted in a 3–1 victory for Argentina. The Netherlands' moment of glory would not come until 1988, when they defeated the Soviet Union in the UEFA Cup championship.

JOHAN CRUYFF

In 1999, Johan Cruyff was voted European Player of the Century. He was also ranked second to Pelé as the World Player of the Century. Born in 1947 in Amsterdam, Cruyff made his debut at age 17 when coach Rinus Michels gave him a place with the club Ajax. (Michels earned FIFA's Coach of the Century Award in 1989.) A disciple of Michels's "total football," Cruyff is legendary because of a move he masterminded known as the "Cruyff turn." Cruyff would look to pass or cross the ball, but then, instead of kicking it, he would drag the ball with the inside of his foot and dribble away, confusing his marker. The Cruyff turn secured a place in soccer lore, and it continues to be copied by players around the world.

MARCO VAN BASTEN

As a player, Marco van Basten was a creative genius, known for perfecting the volley as well as being one of the soccer's greatest all-time forwards. His skill and tactical savvy earned him European Footballer of the Year in 1988, 1989, and 1992.

Van Basten's popularity rose sky-high as a result of his crucial role in the 1988 European Cup championship. In the quarterfinal, he scored a hat trick against England, the winning goal in the semifinal against West Germany, and a stunning volley in the final against the Soviet Union. He was also FIFA World Player of the Year in 1992. Van Basten's playing career ended in 1995 when he was 29 years old. An ankle injury sustained two years earlier, in 1993, had cut his career short. Although Van Basten had always stated that he would never go into management, he became coach of the national team in 2004. He stepped down as coach of the national team after the 2008 European Cup championship.

CHAPTER 10

NIGERIA: FLYING HIGH FOR SOCCER GLORY

Nigeria's passion for soccer bloomed slowly, but the Super Eagles experienced great success in the 1980s and 1990s, a period generally considered to be their golden age. During this time, Nigeria won two African Cup of Nations titles: one in 1980 against Algeria, and one in 1994 against Zambia. The Nigerian national team has won an Olympic gold in addition to their two African Cup of Nations championships.

NICKNAME:
SUPER EAGLES

FEDERATION:
NIGERIA FOOTBALL FEDERATION (NFA)

FOUNDED:
1945

JOINED FIFA:
1960

HONORS:
FIFA WORLD CUP
APPEARANCES: 3
SECOND ROUND IN 1994 AND 1998

AFRICAN CUP OF NATIONS
WINS: 2 (1980, 1994)

FIFA CONFEDERATIONS CUP
APPEARANCES: 1
FOURTH PLACE IN 1995

FIFA U-17 WORLD CUP
WINS: 3
(1985, 1993, 2007)

OLYMPIC MEDAL RECORD
GOLD: 1996 ATLANTA
SILVER: 2008 BEIJING

GETTING THEIR WINGS

The Super Eagles rose to prominence in the 1985 U-17 finals in China, when they beat West Germany. The Germans were unable to keep up with Nigeria's amazing attacking skills and lost by a score of 0–2. At the 1993 FIFA U-17 World Championship in Japan, the Super Eagles scored a 2–1 win against Ghana. Nigerian midfielder Wilson Oruma performed heroically, scoring six goals during the series. In the 2007 U-17 World Championship in South Korea, Nigerian goalkeeper Oladele Ajiboye held strong against Spain in the finals, helping Nigeria win the championship.

Jay-Jay Okocha, one of the greatest African soccer players of all time, blows by Argentine forwards Gabriel Batistuta (left) and Claudio Lopez (right) during the first round of the 2002 World Cup.

Nigerian forward Macauley Chrisantus was awarded the Golden Shoe award for top scorer.

NIGERIA'S GREATEST WINS

Nigeria has done extremely well for a country that is relatively new to international soccer. They won a gold medal after defeating Argentina at the 1996 Olympic Games, in a tournament that's often said to be among the best in Olympic soccer history. Going

Players from Nigeria's national team celebrate their victory over Spain during the final match of the 2007 U-17 World Cup.

into the tournament, the Nigerian team had a reputation for winning at a younger level, with its U-17 titles in 1985 and 1993, and scoring a win at the 1985 U-16 World Tournament. Nigeria was not expected to beat Argentina, but through perseverance, speed, and shooting accuracy, the team triumphed in a 3–2 victory. Nigeria became the first African team ever to win the Olympic gold in soccer. Prior to this victory, European and South American teams had won every gold medal in soccer.

Fast on the heels of another U-17 win in 2007, the Nigerian team, known as "Dream Team IV," won a silver medal at the 2008 Olympics in Beijing after losing to Argentina in the final. Although Nigeria didn't win the gold, this second Olympic medal proved that the Super Eagles have the ability to compete with the best on the international stage.

JAY-JAY OKOCHA

Long before it became a popular sport in Nigeria, midfielder Augustine Azuka "Jay-Jay" Okocha was playing soccer on the streets of his hometown of Enugu, Nigeria. In fact, the only toy he had while growing up was a soccer ball. Okocha became involved in professional soccer while on holiday in Germany celebrating his high school graduation. He visited a club that a friend was playing in and boldly asked the coach if he could train with the rest of the team. At the end of the day, the coach asked him to come back. Okocha was soon signed to the team. An integral part of the golden generation of Nigerian soccer, Okocha is admired for his expert ball-handling skills. He last played for Nigeria at the 2006 CAF African Cup of Nations, where the team placed third.

CHAPTER 11

SPAIN: THE RED FURY

In 1909, Spain created the Royal Spanish Football Federation (RFEF), the national governing body of Spanish soccer. Spain has since become one of the most competitive teams in Europe. Spanish players are known for their extremely fluid attacking style and their thirst to win. There are soccer teams and soccer fields in almost every town in Spain. People follow the public and private lives of players in soccer newspapers, as well as on television and radio shows devoted to the sport.

THE LEGENDARY DI STÉFANO

Alfredo Di Stéfano, a powerful striker for the Spanish national team from 1957 to 1961, was chosen by Pelé as one of the greatest living soccer stars in March 2004. Di Stéfano was famous for his stamina, his incredible technical skills, and his unbelievable versatility, which allowed him to play anywhere on the pitch. As is befitting one of the most talented attacking players in the history of the game (along with Maradona, Cruyff, and Pelé), Di Stéfano was named European Footballer of the Year in 1957 and 1959. He also helped Spain qualify for the World Cup in 1962.

NICKNAME:
LA FURIA ROJA (THE RED FURY)

FEDERATION:
ROYAL SPANISH FOOTBALL FEDERATION (RFEF)

FOUNDED: 1909

JOINED FIFA: 1913

HONORS:
FIFA WORLD CUP
APPEARANCES: 12
FOURTH PLACE IN 1950

UEFA EUROPEAN FOOTBALL CHAMPIONSHIP
APPEARANCES: 8
WINS: 2 (1964, 2008)

FIFA U-20 WORLD CUP
WINS: 1 (1999)

OLYMPIC MEDAL RECORD
GOLD: 1992 BARCELONA
SILVER: 1920 ANTWERP AND 2000 SYDNEY

Spanish forward Emilio Butragueño celebrates after scoring a goal during the 1986 FIFA World Cup. He would score three more goals during the match.

BUTRAGUEÑO: THE VULTURE

Often considered to be one of the greatest Spanish soccer players, Emilio Butragueño was one of the most dangerous strikers in Europe during the 1980s. Nicknamed "the Vulture," Butragueño was always at the center of the team's brilliant counterattacking strategy. Butragueño's greatest accomplishment on the national team is the unbelievable four goals he scored in a single match at the 1986 FIFA World Cup in Mexico.

The proudly victorious Spanish team raises the trophy of the UEFA Euro Cup in June 2008. Spain defeated Germany to win the championship.

2008 UEFA EURO CUP

Aside from winning the gold at the 1992 Olympics in Barcelona, Spain's major claims to fame are their championships in the 1964 and 2008 UEFA Euro Cup tournaments. In the UEFA Euro Cup 2008, Spanish coach Luis Aragones led his team to its first major trophy in 44 years with a 1–0 victory over Germany. Jointly hosted by Austria and Switzerland, the tournament's suspenseful final match took place in Vienna, Austria. An international who's who of politicians, sports heros, musicians, and other celebrities joined the mass of fans at the stadium who witnessed the Spanish triumph. Midfielder Xavi Hernández was named Player of the Tournament by the UEFA. Upon their return to Madrid, the Spanish team was welcomed by tens of thousands of fans and seemingly endless sprays of yellow and red confetti.

CHAPTER 12

THE UNITED STATES:
THE AMERICAN SPIRIT

It's believed that the United States' first soccer team, the Oneida from Boston, Massachusetts, had an official roster of players as far back as 1862. In 1885, the United States was defeated by Canada by a score of 1–0 in the first international game ever played in the Americas. It wasn't until 30 years later, in 1913, that the governing body of U.S. Soccer—the U.S. Football Association (later called the U.S. Soccer Federation)—was formed. In 1914, the United States joined FIFA, and they played their first official international game two years later.

NICKNAME:
RED, WHITE, AND BLUE

FEDERATION:
U.S. SOCCER
FEDERATION (USSF)

FOUNDED:
1913

JOINED FIFA:
1913

HONORS:
FIFA WORLD CUP
APPEARANCES: 8
THIRD PLACE
IN 1930

GOLD CUP
APPEARANCES: 10
WINS: 4 (1991, 2002,
2005, 2007)

FIFA CONFEDERATIONS CUP
APPEARANCES: 3
THIRD PLACE IN 1992
AND 1999

THE GOLD CUP

Although the United States has traditionally been more focused on sports such as baseball, basketball, football, and hockey, the country's national soccer team has slowly become a serious contender on the global soccer circuit. The American team has an impressive tally of CONCACAF Gold Cup appearances from 1991 to 2009, 10, including 4 wins.

The United States stunned the soccer world by becoming the first CONCACAF Gold Cup champion in 1991. They defeated Mexico 2–0 in the semifinals and went on

American soccer superstar Landon Donovan dribbles the ball during the 2002 World Cup, which was hosted by Korea and Japan.

to tie Honduras 0–0 in the final. The U.S. team defeated Honduras 4–3 on penalty kicks in overtime, winning the championship. U.S. goalkeeper Tony Meola, the Gold Cup's first MVP, was spectacular throughout the competition, but he performed especially well in the matches against Mexico and Honduras.

The U.S. team won the 2005 Gold Cup in an exciting final game against Panama. The team's 2007 Gold Cup victory over Mexico was played in front of a sellout crowd of 60,000 fans in Chicago, Illinois.

EARLY SUCCESS

The United States placed third after Argentina and winning team Uruguay in the first ever World Cup tournament, which took place in 1930. During the tournament, U.S. forward Bert Patenaude had the honor of scoring the first hat trick in FIFA World Cup history during a riveting game against Paraguay. According to popular

myth, part of the U.S. team's success was due to the fact that it was mostly made up of former British and Scottish professionals who had immigrated to the United States after the 1928 Olympics.

BRINGING SOCCER FEVER TO THE UNITED STATES

As the United States prepared to host the 1994 World Cup, soccer fans around the world reacted with disbelief—and even some anger. The United States was not considered to have a great soccer tradition, and many worried that no one would actually show up to see the games. The United States was one of the only countries in the world that refers to the sport as "soccer," rather than "football." Could the United States do the game and its fans justice? Soccer fans worldwide were shocked by poll results indicating that not even a quarter of the U.S. population was aware that the tournament was going to be played in their home country. To make matters worse, it seemed that far fewer would even be interested in watching the games, much less buying tickets.

It was in this atmosphere of intense and uncomfortable scrutiny that the games got under way. Soccer followers everywhere were more than ready to criticize FIFA and the United States. Seemingly against all odds, everyone was happily surprised. The games were compelling, dramatic, and drew huge crowds. Although the format was unconventional—the matches were held at various stadiums around the country (including a match at Detroit's Silverdome, the first World Cup match ever played indoors)—the visiting teams and fans were made to feel right at home. The dramatic final between Brazil and Italy was staged at the Rose Bowl in Pasadena, California, on July 17, 1994. Though the U.S. team failed to place, the games were a triumph: television ratings skyrocketed past the most hopeful predictions, profits were high, and perhaps the most important of all was the birth of a new nation of soccer fanatics—the United States.

African Cup of Nations Begun in 1957 and held every two years, the African Cup of Nations is a competition for teams who compete in the African Football Confederation (CAF).

cap A recognition given to a player for every appearance in an international game for his or her country.

Confederation of African Football (CAF) The administration that organizes soccer in Africa.

Confederation of North, Central American and Caribbean Association Football (CONCACAF) The governing body that organizes soccer in North America, Central America, and the Caribbean.

Confederations Cup A competition between the six winning countries of each of the six confederations of world soccer, the current FIFA World Cup winner, and the host country. It is played the year before the FIFA World Cup.

Copa América Begun in 1916, it is the oldest international soccer competition. The teams that compete for this trophy are in the South American Confederation (CONMEBOL). It is usually held every two years.

dribbling Moving the soccer ball under close control with a series of taps or short kicks.

FIFA U-17 World Cup An international competition for players 17 years old or younger. It is held every two years.

FIFA U-20 World Cup A world cup for players 20 years old or younger. It is held every two years.

Gold Cup Begun in 1961, this is a competition for national teams in CONCACAF. It is held every two years.

hat trick When three goals are scored by a player in one game.

midfielder The player who links together the offensive and defensive functions of a team. Midfielders play behind their forwards.

rivalry An intense, prolonged competition between two opposing teams or players.

sweeper A defender who can play closest to the goal, behind the other defenders, or as an attacker responsible for advancing the ball forward.

UEFA The Union of European Football Associations, which controls soccer in Europe.

UEFA European Football Championship Also known as EURO Cup. Teams from the UEFA compete for this trophy. It takes place once every four years.

volley Any ball kicked by a player when it's off the ground.

FOR MORE INFORMATION

AYSO National Support & Training Center
12501 S. Isis Avenue
Hawthorne, CA 90250
(800) 872-2976
(310) 643-5310
Web site: http://soccer.org/home.aspx
The American Youth Soccer Organization (AYSO) is a nonprofit organization that runs youth soccer programs all over the country.

Canadian Soccer Association
Place Soccer Canada
237 rue Metcalfe Street
K2P 1R2
Ottawa, ON
Canada
(613) 237-7678
Web site: http://www.canadasoccer.com
The Canadian Soccer Association provides information on Canada's national soccer team, profiles of players and competitions, and FIFA competitions.

CONCACAF
725 Fifth Avenue, Floor 17
New York, NY 10022
(212) 308-0044
Web site: http://www.concacaf.com
This administrative body organizes soccer in North America, Central America, and the Caribbean.

National Soccer Hall of Fame
18 Stadium Circle
Oneonta, NY 13820
(607) 432-3351

Web site: http://www.soccerhall.org
The National Soccer Hall of Fame has a museum dedicated to soccer in the United States.

U.S. Soccer Federation
1801 S. Prairie Avenue
Chicago, IL 60616
(312) 808-1300
Web site: http://www.ussoccer.com
The U.S. Soccer Federation is the governing body of soccer in the United States.

U.S. Soccer Foundation
1211 Connecticut Avenue NW, Suite 500
Washington, DC 20036
(202) 872-9277
Web site: http://www.ussoccerfoundation.org
The U.S. Soccer Foundation provides grants and soccer equipment to programs in underserved areas, and gives young people an opportunity to experience the game.

WEB SITES

Due to the changing nature of Internet links, Rosen Publishing has developed an online list of Web sites related to the subject of this book. This site is updated regularly. Please use this link to access the list:

http://www.rosenlinks.com/wsb/natl

FOR FURTHER READING

Bloor, Edward. *Tangerine*. Boston, MA: Houghton Mifflin Harcourt, 2008.

Branner, Toni. *The Care and Feeding of a Soccer Player: Find and Exceed Your Potential on the Field*. Houston, TX: Blue Water Press, 2007.

Buckley, James. *Pelé*. New York, NY: DK Children, 2007.

Buxton, Ted. *Soccer Skills: For Young Players*. Buffalo, NY: Firefly Books, 2007.

Coleman, Lori. *Girls Soccer: Going for the Goal*. Mankato, MN: Coughlan Publishing, 2007.

Crisfiel, Deborah. *Winning Soccer for Girls*. New York, NY: Checkmark Books, 2009.

Dorrance, Anson. *The Vision of a Champion: Advice and Inspiration from the World's Most Successful Soccer Coach*. Ann Arbor, MI: Huron River Press, 2005.

Fitzgerald, Dawn. *Soccer Chick Rules*. New York, NY: Square Fish, 2007.

Gifford, Clive. *The Kingfisher Soccer Encyclopedia*. Boston, MA: Kingfisher Books, 2006.

Goldblatt, David. *The Ball Is Round: A Global History of Soccer*. New York, NY: Riverhead, 2008.

Gutman, Dan. *The Million Dollar Kick*. New York, NY: Hyperion Books for Children, 2006.

Hornby, Hugh. *Soccer*. New York, NY: DK Eyewitness Books, 2008.

Hunt, Chris. *The Complete Book of Soccer*. Buffalo, NY: Firefly Books 2006.

Koger, Robert. *101 Great Youth Soccer Drills*. New York, NY: McGraw Hill, 2005.

Morris, Christopher. *Soccer: From Beckham to Zidane*. New York, NY: Simon & Schuster, 2008.

Rigby, Robert. *Goal: The Dream Begins*. Boston, MA: Harcourt Paperbacks, 2006.

St. John, Warren. *Outcasts United: A Refugee Team, an American Town*. New York, NY: Spiegal & Grau, 2009.

Saunders, Catherine, ed. *Soccer: The Ultimate Guide*. New York, NY: DK Publishing, 2008.

Shea, Teresa. *Soccer Stars*. New York, NY: Children's Press, 2007.

Spring, Debbie. *Breathing Soccer*. Markham, Ontario: Fitzhenry & Whiteside, Ltd., 2008.

Stewart, Mark. *The World Cup*. New York, NY: Franklin Watts (Scholastic), 2003.

Tigelaar, Liz. *PrettyTOUGH*. New York, NY: Razorbill; Penguin Young Readers Group, 2007.

Wangerin, David. *Soccer in a Football World: The Story of America's Forgotten Game*. Philadelphia, PA: Temple University Press 2008.

Wilson, Johnathan. *Inverting the Pyramid: The History of Football Tactics*. London, England: Orion, 2008.

Africa Online. "Essien, Adebayo Arrive for GLO-CAF Awards." February 10, 2009. Retrieved March 13, 2009 (http://www.afriquejet.com/news/africa-news).

BBC Sport. "BBC Sport's Euro 2008 Guide to the Netherlands." May 15, 2008. Retrieved March 19, 2009 (http://www.news.bbc.co.uk).

BBC Sport. "Death Heart Related." July 7, 2003. Retrieved March 13, 2009 (http://news.bbc.co.uk/sport2).

BBC Sport. "Lippi Resigns as Italy Head Coach." July 12, 2006. Retrieved March 20, 2009 (http://news.bbc.co.uk/sport2/hi/football/world_cup_2006).

BBC Sport. "USA Continues Domination with 2–1 Victory Over Mexico to Lift Fourth Overall CONCACAF Gold Cup Trophy." June 24, 2007. Retrieved March 21, 2009 (http://news.bbc.co.uk/sport2/hi/football).

CAF. "CAF Release 30 Best African Players in the Last 50 Years." November 8, 2007. Retrieved March 17, 2009 (http://www.cafonline.com).

CAF. "Dicey Away Duels for Former Africa Champions." March 27, 2009. Retrieved March 27, 2009 (http://www.cafonline.com/competition/african-cup-of-nations).

Chapin, Mark. "UEFO Praises the Friendly Finals." June 30, 2008. Retrieved March 27, 2009 (http://www1.uefa.com/news/kind=1/newsid=729426.html#uefa+praises+friendly+finals).

Etonge, Martin. "State Funeral for Foe." Retrieved March 25, 2009 (http://www.ussoccer.com/articles).

Euro2008.com. "World's Best Bring Madrid to Standstill." June 30, 2008. Retrieved March 16, 2009 (http://en.euro2008.uefa.com/news/kind=1/newsid=729558.html#worlds+best+bring+madrid+standstill).

FIFA.com. "Argentina Thrives on Maradona Factor." March 27, 2009. Retrieved March 29, 2009 (http://www.fifa.com/worldcup/news/news).

FIFA.com. "Beckham Equals England Record." February 12, 2009. Retrieved March 23, 2009 (http://www.fifa.com/worldfootball/news).

FIFA.com. "Charlton Given Freedom of Manchester." Retrieved March 2, 2009 (http://www.fifa.com/worldfootball/clubfootball/news).

FIFA.com. "Honduran Joy and Mexican Pain." November 20, 2008. Retrieved March 21, 2009 (http://www.fifa.com/worldcup/news).

FIFA.com. "Marquez: Don't Blame Me." Retrieved March 23, 2009 (http://www.fifa.com).

FIFA.com. "Moves That Made History." January 11, 2007. Retrieved March 25, 2009 (http://www.fifa.com/worldfootball/news).

FIFA.com. "A New Look for Cameroon." March 17, 2009. Retrieved March 20, 2009 (http://www.fifa.com).

Goal.com. "Dunga Gives Ronaldinho Total Freedom in Brazil Team." March 27, 2009. Retrieved March 30, 2009 (http://www.goal.com).

Lalas, George. "Egypt Beats Cameroon 1–0; Wins 6th Title." February 10, 2008. Retrieved March 17, 2009 (http://www.iht.com/articles/2008).

Omary, Majuto. "Tanzania/Cameroon: Football Federation Unveils Entrance Fees." *The Citizen*, June 4, 2008. Retrieved March 13, 2009 (http://allafrica.com/stories).

Vubem, Fred. "Nigeria/Cameroon: CAF Awards Today in Nigeria." *Cameroon Tribune*, February 10, 2009. Retrieved March 15, 2009 (http://allafrica.com/stories/200902100604.html).

World Soccer magazine. "Brian Glanville on the Ugly Side of Italian Football." March 25, 2009. Retrieved March 28, 2009 (http://www.worldsoccer.com/news).

ABOUT THE AUTHOR

Annie Leah Sommers is a writer and editor based in New York. She holds a BA in English literature from McGill University in Montreal, an MA in children's literature from the Center for the Study of Children's Literature at Simmons College in Boston, and a secondary school teaching diploma in English and ESL from McGill University. She was in Paris, France, for the FIFA World Cup in 1998.

PHOTO CREDITS

Cover, p. 1 (top) John Thys/AFP/Getty Images; cover, p. 1 (bottom), pp. 7, 9, 11–12, 13, 15–16, 19–20, 23–24, 27–28, 31–32, 35–36, 39–40, 43–44, 47–48, 51–52, 55–56 © www.istockphoto. com/Roberta Casaliggi; pp. 14, 29, 54–55 © Popperfoto/Getty Images; p. 5 © Newscom; p. 8 © Guillermo Mu-Oz/AFP/Getty Images; p. 10 © Diego Maradona/Arg Foto/Bongarts/Getty Images; pp. 12–13, 18, 38, 42 © Bob Thomas/Getty Images; p. 17 © Martin Bureau/AFP/Getty Images; p. 21 © Mary Evans Picture Library/The Image Works; p. 22 © AP Photos; p. 25 © Getty Images; p. 26 © Patrick Hertzog/AFP/Getty Images; p. 30 © Steve Munday/Allsport/Getty Images; p. 33 © Sandra Behne/Bongarts/Getty Images; pp. 34, 41 © AFP/Getty Images; p. 37 © Jaime Razuri/AFP/Getty Images; p. 45 © Toshifumi Kitamura/AFP/Getty Images; p. 46 © Choi Won-Suk/AFP/Getty Images; p. 49 © Joel Robine/Getty Images; p. 50 © Denis Doyle/Getty Images; p. 53 © Andreas Rentz/Getty Images.

Designer: Matthew Cauli; Photo Researcher: Marty Levick